I Can Cook!

AMERICAN FOOD

Wendy Blaxland

A+

Smart Apple Media
P.O. Box 3263
Mankato, MN, 56002

Reprinted 2012

First published in 2011 by
MACMILLAN EDUCATION AUSTRALIA PTY LTD
15–19 Claremont St, South Yarra, Australia 3141

Visit our website at www.macmillan.com.au or go directly to www.macmillanlibrary.com.au

Associated companies and representatives throughout the world.

Copyright text © Wendy Blaxland 2011

Library of Congress Cataloging-in-Publication Data

Blaxland, Wendy.
    American food / Wendy Blaxland.
        p. cm. — (I can cook!)
    Includes index.
    Summary:"Describes historical, cultural, and geographical factors that have influenced the cuisine of the United States.
    Includes recipes to create American food"—Provided by publisher.
    ISBN 978-1-59920-667-7 (library binding)
    1. Cooking, American—Juvenile literature. 2. Food—United States—History—Juvenile literature. 3. Cookbooks. I. Title.
    TX715.B6392 2012
641.5973—dc22
                        2011005443

Publisher: Carmel Heron
Commissioning Editor: Niki Horin
Managing Editor: Vanessa Lanaway
Editor: Laura Jeanne Gobal
Proofreaders: Georgina Garner; Kirstie Innes–Will
Designer: Stella Vassiliou
Page Layout: Stella Vassiliou
Photo Researcher: Claire Armstrong (management: Debbie Gallagher)
Illustrators: Jacki Sosenko; Guy Holt (map, **7**, **9**); Gregory Baldwin (map icons, **9**)
Production Controller: Vanessa Johnson

Manufactured in China by Macmillan Production (Asia) Ltd.
Kwun Tong, Kowloon, Hong Kong
Supplier Code: CP March 2011

Acknowledgments
The author would like to thank the following for their generous help and expert advice: Emeritus Professor Eugene Anderson, University of California; Alison Barnard, Consulate General of the United States of America; Emily Gelsomin, dietitian, Boston; Peter Gilbert, US Reference Service, Sydney; Michael Jarvis and Craig Morris, US Department of Agriculture; Linni Kral, food writer, Boston; Betty Ollen, cook and food writer, Boston; Wayne Olson, reference librarian, US National Agricultural Library; Lynne Olver, editor, FoodTimeline; Jennifer Porter, US Department of Agriculture; Professor Barbara Santich, University of Adelaide; Barbara Rotger, Melrose; Dena Saulsbury-Monaco, cook and librarian, Montreal; and Michael Sheats, US Department of Agriculture.

The author and the publisher are grateful to the following for permission to reproduce copyright material:

Front cover photograph: Hamburger courtesy of Shutterstock/Lilyana Vynogradova.
Back cover photographs: Rye bread courtesy of Dreamstime/Olgalis; brown paper bag courtesy of Shutterstock/Nils Z; sourdough bread courtesy of Shutterstock/Janet Faye Hastings; hamburger courtesy of Shutterstock/Dan Peretz; and corn courtesy of Shutterstock/Anna Subbotina.

Photographs courtesy of: Dreamstime/Olgalis, **6** (rye), /Yukata, **15** (muffins); Getty Images/Ligia Botero, **25** (lemonade jug & glasses), /Annabelle Breakey, **30** (center), /Comstock Images, **29**, /Valerie Janssen, **19** (top center), /Joe Kohen, **28**; iStockphoto.com/ajafoto, **10** (tea towel), /Gary Alvis, **15** (blueberries), /brinkstock, **13** (clipboard), /FreezeFrameStudio, **30** (bottom), /gbh007, **4** (right), /gerisima, **6** (suitcase), /gojak, **24** (lemon slices), **25** (lemon slices), /Robyn Mac, **10** (hanging utensils), /MorePixels, **21** (top left), /Urosh Petrovic, **throughout** (red oven mitt), /RedHelga, **14** (blueberries); Photolibrary/Imagesource, **5** (right), /Juan Manuel Silva, **23** (pancake stack); Shutterstock/Aaron Amat, **4–5** (chocolate splash), **11** (grater), /Ambrophoto, **8** (oranges), /Anat-oli, **9** (pig), /Anson0618, **8** (rice), /Mark Aplet, **13** (electric mixer), **31**, /Hamiza Bakirci, **8** (strawberries),/Adrian Britton, **10** (baking tray), /Darren Brode, **11** (electric mixer), /Ilker Canikligil, **10** (saucepan), **13** (saucepan), /Norman Chan, **8** (clams), /ZH Chen, **10** (measuring cups), /Cathleen A Clapper, **7** (bottom right), /Coprid, **13** (soap dispenser), /Luis Francisco Cordero, **10** (whisk), /Mikael Damkier, **10** (frying pan, measuring jug), /Raphael Daniaud, **11** (blender), /ejwhite, **11** (colander), /Freddy Eliasson, **7** (center), /Elkostas, **8** (lettuce), /Christopher Elwell, **9** (oats), /Iakov Filimonov, **13** (knives), /Kellie L. Folkerts, **8** (milk), /Gilmanshin, **13** (knife block), /Givaga, **8** (salmon), /gjfoto, **8** (pork), /Gordan Gledec, **8** (sweet potatoes), /gresei, **9** (walnuts), /grublee, **17** (tomatoes), /Janet Faye Hastings, **6** (sourdough), **8** (mixed salad), /HL Photo, **7** (top left), /Oliver Hoffmann, **8** (kidney beans), /Jiang Hongyan, **23** (eggs), /Bogdan Ionescu, **8** (whole pumpkin), /Tischenko Irina, **10** (fruit & veg), **10** (large knife, butter knife), /Eric Isselée, **9** (cow), /Ivaylo Ivanov, **9** (rice), /K13 ART, **11** (blue bowl), **11** (bowls), /Kamira, **8** (bread), /Kayros Studio, **13** (fire extinguisher), /Krasowit, **9** (fish), /Elena Larina, **19** (peanuts), /LazarevDN, **10** (sieve), /Chris Leachman, **10** (chopping board), /Rudchenko Liliia, **8** (beef), /Louella938, **9** (pecans), /Olga Lyubkina, **8** (chicken), /Petr Malyshev, **13** (kettle), /Iain McGillivray, **10** (tongs), /Basov Mikhail, **8** (cheese, center), /Mongolka, **8** (pineapple), /Monkey Business Images, **7** (top right), /Mopic, **13** (first-aid box), /Nattika, **8** (apples), **26** (whole apples), **27** (apples), /Paul Paladin, **8** (cheese, right), /Dan Peretz, **17** (top center), /Peter Polak, **8** (mixed beans), /Ragnarock, **11** (slotted spoon), **13** (frying pan), /Stephen Aaron Rees, **11** (wooden spoon), /Sally Scott, **8** (blueberries), /Smit, **8** (spinach), /David P. Smith, **27** (top left), /soncerina, **10** (fork), /stanislaff, **8** (tortillas), /STILLFX, **10** (peeler), /Anna Subbotina, **6** (corn), **20** (top left), **21** (top right), /tatniz, **8** (watermelon), /testing, **20** (corn kernels), **21** (corn kernels), /Ev Thomas, **13** (fire blanket), /JR Trice, **6** (cornbread), /Analia Valeria Urani, **7** (bottom left), /Matt Valentine, **10** (bread knife), /GraÃ§a Victoria, **10** (oven mitts), **13** (oven mitts), /Vlue, **10** (steak knife), /Valentyn Volkov, **23** (honey), /Brian Weed, **8** (cheese, left), /Feng Yu, **17** (mustard), /zcw, **8** (halved pumpkin), /Dusan Zidar, **30** (top).

Contents

Glossary Words

When a word is printed in **bold**, it is explained in the Glossary on page 31.

Cooking Tips

Safety Warning

Ask an adult for help when you see this red oven mitt on a recipe.

How To

Cooking techniques are explained in small boxes with this handprint.

I Can Cook!

Cooking is a rewarding and lifelong skill. With some basic cooking knowledge, a little practice, and great recipes, you can cook entire meals! Cooking for your family and friends is a fun activity, and a mouthwatering meal can take you to places that you have never been. Are you ready to have fun cooking—and eating?

A World of Food

Every day, people all over the world cook delicious and **nutritious** meals. What they cook depends not only on the ingredients available to them, but also on their country's food **culture** or cooking style. A country's style of cooking is shaped over time by its culture, **economy**, **climate**, and the land itself.

Cook Your Way Around the World

You can explore the great cuisines of the world in your own kitchen. The special flavors and wonderful aromas of a country's food culture come from fresh ingredients and particular spices or herbs, which you can find in your local supermarket or a specialty store. Share with your family and friends authentic dishes from different countries that look great and taste even better.

You can cook mouth-watering food from different countries by following a few simple steps. Some recipes involve combining just a couple of ingredients!

American Food

The food Americans eat is influenced by our country's history and landscape—where our families originally came from, which part of the country we live in, and what ingredients are available there.

Many Different Foods

American cuisine varies widely, from sweet apple pies to spicy chili dishes, because the United States (U.S.) has a range of climates, landscapes, and local cooking **traditions**. Americans come from many different countries and backgrounds as well.

Cooking American Food at Home

American food is easy to cook at home. This book has seven recipes that you can follow to cook a meal on your own or with a little help from an adult. Some of the recipes don't even involve cooking. They can be adapted to suit special **diets**, too.

NORTH AMERICA

UNITED STATES OF AMERICA

Alaska

Hawaii

SOUTH AMERICA

EUROPE

ASIA

AFRICA

AUSTRALIA

N

America is known officially as the United States of America because it consists of fifty states. These states are all located on the North American **continent**, except the islands of Hawaii.

Milkshakes are a popular American drink you can make at home by combining milk and ice cream or iced milk with flavorings, such as chocolate syrup.

Traditions and Styles

The traditions and styles of American cooking are a result of the **migration** of millions of people from different cultures to America. This happened over hundreds of years and has led to a varied cuisine.

American bread includes corn bread (center) inspired by Native American cooking, sourdough (left) from British cooking traditions, and rye (right) from the Germans.

Early American Food

Native American cooking was based on corn, beans, and pumpkins, which were found only in America. Native Americans also hunted wild animals, caught fish, and gathered fruit. They taught the first migrants, who arrived in the early 1600s mainly from the United Kingdom (U.K.), how to use these local ingredients.

The Influence of Mass Migration

From the early 1700s, Africans brought to America as **slaves** cooked the fried and spicy food they loved on plantations and, later, on the railroads. In the late 1800s, migrants from all over northern Europe brought their taste for meat, potatoes, and baked goods. Then, at the beginning of the 1900s, more migrants poured in from southern and eastern Europe with a whole range of cooking styles. **Latin Americans** also added their distinctive flavors. As different cooking styles merged, a new cuisine was formed—American food.

Regional Food

Every region in the U.S. offers special dishes linked to the cooking styles of the migrants who settled there. The map below breaks America up into five main regions and discusses the ingredients and special foods that are popular in each.

Northwest
Recipes here are often meat-based because of the many cattle ranches in the area. Areas along the Pacific coast use berries and fish, such as salmon (pictured) and trout.

Southwest
Native American and Mexican influences led to the development of barbecued meats (pictured), along with spicy chili bean and meat recipes.

Northeast
Apple pie was developed from British cooking styles. Dutch and Scandinavian migrants introduced fruit cobblers and pies (pictured), and Danish pastries. Italian and central European migrants brought pizzas, bagels, and dill pickles.

Southeast
Sweet potato pie and collard greens evolved from the simple cooking of African slaves. Gumbo (pictured), a rich stew, stems from Cajun and Creole cooking, both of which have French origins.

Midwest
Midwestern food includes thin Swedish pancakes, German pork sausages, and Polish *pierogi* (dumplings, pictured).

Map labels: CANADA, Great Plains, NORTHWEST, West Coast, MEXICO, Pacific Ocean, Alaska, SOUTHWEST, SOUTHEAST, MIDWEST, NORTHEAST, Gulf of Mexico

7

American Food Basics

American Ingredients

The U.S. is a huge country that can grow many types of fruit and vegetables, and raise a variety of animals for their meat. This means Americans have a wide selection of ingredients to use when cooking.

Meat
Americans love cooking with meat, especially beef, pork, and chicken.

Seafood
Waters along the American coasts provide fish, such as salmon, and other seafood, including clams and lobsters, for the whole country.

Dairy Products
Milk and cheese are found in many American recipes.

Fruit
American recipes use a variety of fruit, including strawberries, blueberries, apples, oranges, watermelons, and pineapples.

Staple Foods
Bread, made from wheat flour, is a **staple food** of the American diet. Rice and corn are also popular, especially in the south, where tortillas are made from cornmeal.

Vegetables
Popular vegetables include sweet potatoes, pumpkins, and beans. Green salads are also common.

Landscapes and Climates

The landscapes of the U.S. range from deserts, **swamps** and **fertile** river plains in the south, to high mountain ranges and flat central plains, and coastal plains and lakes. The country's climates also vary from the cold north, to milder and warm central areas, and hot southern areas. The map below shows the food produced in various areas of the U.S.

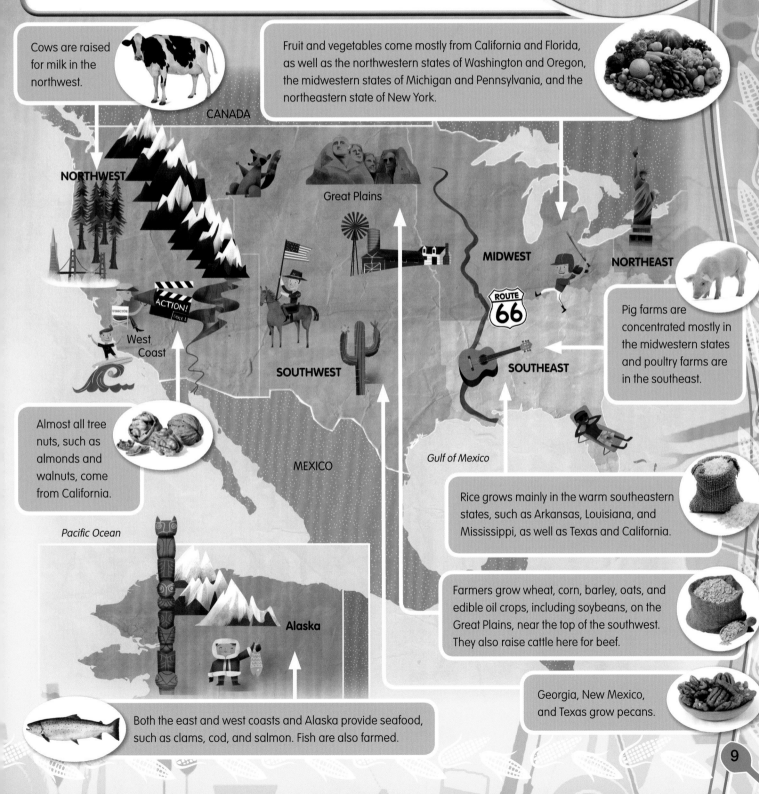

Cows are raised for milk in the northwest.

Fruit and vegetables come mostly from California and Florida, as well as the northwestern states of Washington and Oregon, the midwestern states of Michigan and Pennsylvania, and the northeastern state of New York.

CANADA

NORTHWEST

Great Plains

MIDWEST

NORTHEAST

ROUTE 66

SOUTHWEST

SOUTHEAST

West Coast

Pig farms are concentrated mostly in the midwestern states and poultry farms are in the southeast.

Almost all tree nuts, such as almonds and walnuts, come from California.

Pacific Ocean

MEXICO

Gulf of Mexico

Alaska

Rice grows mainly in the warm southeastern states, such as Arkansas, Louisiana, and Mississippi, as well as Texas and California.

Farmers grow wheat, corn, barley, oats, and edible oil crops, including soybeans, on the Great Plains, near the top of the southwest. They also raise cattle here for beef.

Georgia, New Mexico, and Texas grow pecans.

Both the east and west coasts and Alaska provide seafood, such as clams, cod, and salmon. Fish are also farmed.

9

Cooking Basics

Equipment

Having the right equipment to cook with is very important. Here are some of the most common items needed in the kitchen.

Potato mashers break up food.

Sieves separate and break up food.

Spatulas lift and turn food.

Cook pasta, rice, soups, and stews in saucepans.

Big knives chop. Small knives cut and peel. Butter knives spread. Serrated knives slice.

Oven mitts protect hands from heat.

Baking pans hold food in an oven.

Forks hold, stir, or prick food.

Whisks beat food to add air and make it light.

Tongs are used to handle hot food.

Measuring cups and spoons measure ingredients accurately.

Frying pans fry or brown food.

Peelers remove the skins from fruit and vegetables.

Cutting boards provide safe surfaces for cutting food.

Blenders chop ingredients, mix food, and make smooth sauces and soups.

Spoons mix and stir. Wooden spoons prevent scratched pans. Slotted spoons let liquid drain away.

Graters shave thin slices from food, such as cheese.

Colanders drain liquids.

Mixers mix food quickly.

Bowls hold food for mixing.

Cooking Basics

Weight, Volume, Temperature, and Special Diets

It is important to use the right amount of ingredients, cook at the correct heat, and be aware of people with special dietary needs.

Weight and Volume

The weight and volume of ingredients can be measured with a weighing scale or with measuring cups and spoons. Convert them using this table. Measure dry ingredients so that they are level across the top of the spoon or cup without packing them down.

Recipe Measurement	Weight	Volume
1 cup	8 ounces	250 ml
½ cup	4 ounces	125 ml
2 tablespoons	1 ounce	30 ml
1 teaspoon	0.16 ounce	4.7 ml

Temperature

Fahrenheit and Celsius are two different ways of measuring temperature. Oven dials may show the temperature in either Fahrenheit or Celsius. Use lower temperatures in gas or convection ovens.

Oven Temperature	Celsius	Fahrenheit
Slow	150°	300°
Moderately slow	160°–170°	320°–340°
Moderate	180°	350°
Moderately hot	190°	375°
Hot	200°	400°
Very hot	220°–240°	430°–470°

Special Diets

Some people follow special diets because of personal or religious beliefs about what they should eat. Others must not eat certain foods because they are **allergic** to them.

Diet	What It Means	Symbol
Allergy-specific	Some people's bodies react to a certain food as if it were poison. They may die from eating even a tiny amount of this food. Nuts, eggs, milk, strawberries, and even chocolate may cause allergic reactions.	
Halal	**Muslims** eat only food prepared according to strict religious guidelines. This is called halal food.	
Kosher	**Jews** eat only food prepared according to strict religious guidelines. This is called kosher food.	
Vegan	Vegans eat nothing from animals, including dairy products, eggs, and honey.	
Vegetarian	Vegetarians eat no animal products and may or may not eat dairy products, eggs, and honey.	

Safety and Hygiene

Be safe in the kitchen by staying alert and using equipment correctly when cooking. Practicing good food hygiene means you always serve clean, germ-free food. Follow the handy tips below!

Be Organized

Hungry? Organized cooks eat sooner! First, read the recipe. Next, take out the equipment and ingredients you'll need and follow the stages set out in the recipe. Straighten up and clean as you go. While your food cooks, wash up, sweep the kitchen floor, and empty the garbage.

Heat

Place boiling saucepans toward the back of the stove with handles turned inward. Keep your hands and face away from steam and switch hot equipment off as soon as you have finished using it. Use oven mitts to pick up hot pots and put them down on heatproof surfaces. Always check that food is cool enough to eat.

Emergencies

All kitchens should have a fire blanket, fire extinguisher, and first-aid box.

Food Hygiene

To avoid spreading germs, wash your hands well and keep coughs and sneezes away from food. Use fresh ingredients and always store food that spoils easily, such as meat and fish, in the refrigerator.

Electricity

Use electrical equipment only with an adult's help. Switch the power off before unplugging any equipment, and keep it away from water.

Knives

When cutting food with a knife, cut away from yourself and onto a nonslip surface, such as a suitable cutting board.

Blueberry Muffins

Muffins in the U.S. were originally flat, round English muffins. In the 1900s, American cake-like muffins using fruit, such as native blueberries, became popular, along with savory varieties that used ham or pumpkin. Muffins are generally eaten for breakfast in the U.S.

MAKES: 6 muffins

PREPARATION TIME: 10 minutes

COOKING TIME: 20 minutes

FOOD VALUES: About 135 **calories**, 5 grams of fat, 3 grams of **protein**, and 20 grams of **carbohydrates** per muffin.

SPECIAL DIETS: Suitable for vegetarian, nut-free, kosher, and halal diets. For **gluten**-free diets, use gluten-free flour; for vegan diets use ½ a ripe, mashed banana instead of an egg and use soy, rice, or coconut milk or juice instead of dairy milk.

Equipment

- 6 paper muffin cups
- Muffin pan
- Colander
- 2 mixing bowls
- Wooden spoon
- Tablespoon
- Toothpick or skewer

Ingredients

- 1 cup of blueberries (fresh or frozen)
- 1¾ cups of self-rising flour
- 3 tablespoons of sugar
- 1 egg
- 1 cup of milk
- 3 tablespoons of vegetable oil (canola or sunflower)

Recipe Variations

Use 3 tablespoons of honey instead of sugar for a different taste and only ⅔ a cup of milk.

What to Do

1

400°F

Preheat the oven to 400°F.

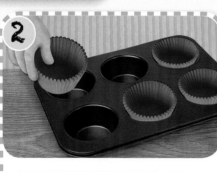

2

Place the muffin cups in the muffin pan. Rinse the fresh blueberries, drain, and set them aside.

3

Mix the flour and sugar in a bowl. Add the blueberries and **fold** them gently into the mixture.

Ask an adult for help with using the oven.

How To: Fold

Scatter the blueberries on the dry mixture. Next, use the wooden spoon to gently lift the ingredients from the bottom of the bowl to the top, "folding" the ingredients together. Repeat until the blueberries and dry mixture are combined.

How To: Beat

Mix the milk, oil, and egg very quickly with the wooden spoon until completely combined.

4

Crack the egg into another bowl. Add the milk and oil to the egg and **beat** well.

5

Combine the two mixtures until they are just mixed. Do not over-mix.

6

Fill the muffin cups about ⅔ full with the mixture and cook for 20 minutes in the oven.

7

Five minutes before time's up, test that the muffins are cooked by sticking a toothpick or skewer into a muffin. If it comes out clean, the muffins are ready. Let the muffins cool in the pan.

Hamburgers

In the early 1800s, German migrants introduced a seasoned ground beef dish to the U.S. This dish came to be known as "beef steak à la Hamburg," named after the German city of Hamburg. The hamburger evolved from this dish but became popular only in 1921, when a fast-food restaurant advertised their five-cent burgers as clean and safe. Today, Americans eat billions of hamburgers every year!

MAKES: 2 hamburgers

PREPARATION TIME: 15 minutes

COOKING TIME: 5 minutes

FOOD VALUES: About 225 calories, 9 g of fat, 30 g of protein, and 8 g of carbohydrates per hamburger.

SPECIAL DIETS: Suitable for nut-free and dairy-free diets. For vegetarian and vegan diets, use vegetarian patties; for gluten-free diets, use gluten-free buns; for kosher and halal diets, use certified ingredients.

Equipment

- Spatula
- Cutting board
- Small, sharp knife
- Frying pan
- Paper towels
- Butter knife
- Serving plate

Ingredients

- ½ pound of lean ground meat
- 2 buns or bread rolls
- ½ of a tomato
- 2 teaspoons of vegetable oil (canola or sunflower)
- Margarine (or butter) or mayonnaise
- 2 rinsed lettuce leaves
- 2 slices of pickle
- Ketchup, to taste
- Mustard, to taste

What to Do

1. Shape the meat into 2 equally sized balls and flatten them to form 2 round patties.

2. Halve the buns. Cut the tomato into thin slices.

3. Cook the patties for 3 minutes in the oil in the frying pan at high heat. Do not press the patties down (pressing them will release the flavor). Turn the patties with a spatula. Cook them for another 2 minutes.

Recipe Variations

After turning each patty, add a slice of cheese to melt it slightly. Vegans may add sliced avocado or beet slices instead.

Try breads such as pita, tortilla, or focaccia instead of buns.

Ask an adult for help with using the knife and stove.

4 Check that the patties are cooked by making a small cut to the middle of one patty. If it is still pink inside, cook the patties for another 30 seconds. Use paper towels to blot the fat from the patties.

5 Toast the buns. Spread margarine or mayonnaise on the bottom half of each bun. Place one patty on each half.

6 Top the patties with lettuce, pickle, tomato slices, ketchup, and mustard. Cover with the remaining halves of the buns.

Peanut Butter and Jelly Sandwich

The invention of sliced, packaged bread in the 1920s meant that children could make sandwiches themselves. Cheap but filling peanut butter and jelly sandwiches became popular during the hard times of the 1930s. Today, the average American eats about 1,500 "PB&J" sandwiches before finishing high school!

MAKES: 1 sandwich

PREPARATION TIME: 2 minutes

FOOD VALUES: About 280 calories, 10 g of fat, 9 g of protein, and 30 g of carbohydrates per sandwich.

SPECIAL DIETS: Suitable for vegan, vegetarian, kosher, and halal diets. For nut-free diets, try another spread, such as tahini, a sesame seed spread. For gluten-free diets, use gluten-free bread.

Recipe Variations

Toast the bread before spreading the peanut butter and jelly on it.

Try honey, bananas, or dried fruit instead of jelly.

Equipment

- Cutting board
- Butter knife

Ingredients

- 2 slices of bread
- 1 tablespoon of peanut butter
- 1 tablespoon of jelly spread

What to Do

Use the knife to spread the peanut butter over one slice of bread.

Spread the jelly over the remaining slice of bread.

3 Place one slice of bread on top of the other, so that the peanut butter and jelly touch.

4 Cut the sandwich in half.

Corn on the Cob

Native Americans taught the first British settlers, known as the Pilgrims, how to grow corn, an important food that was eaten at the first Thanksgiving. It is now America's largest crop. Corn on the cob is a sweet variety of corn that is picked unripe to roast or boil.

MAKES: 1 ear of corn

PREPARATION TIME: 5 minutes

COOKING TIME: stove—15 minutes; microwave—5 minutes

FOOD VALUES: About 77 calories, 1 g of fat, 3 g of protein, and 17 g of carbohydrates per ear of corn.

SPECIAL DIETS: Suitable for vegan, vegetarian, nut-free, gluten-free, kosher, and halal diets.

Equipment

- Tongs
- Saucepan big enough to fit the ear of corn
- Serving plate
- Butter knife

Ingredients

- 1 fresh ear of corn (husk on)
- 1 teaspoon of butter or margarine (optional)

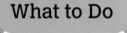

What to Do

1 Microwave: Place the corn on the microwave's turntable. Cook it for 1 minute on high. If the corn kernels still look shiny and firm, cook the corn for another 30 seconds on high.

2 Use tongs to remove the corn from the microwave. Let it cool on the plate. Next, strip the corn of its husk by pulling it downward, as if you were peeling a banana (see step 3). Jump to step 6.

3 Stove: Strip the corn of its husk, which is the outer covering of leaves and the silky threads beneath it.

Recipe Variations

Dust the corn with a little chilli powder before serving.

Cut the corn kernels off the cob and eat them separately.

Ask an adult for help with using the stove or microwave.

4

Pour enough cold water into the saucepan to cover the corn. Bring the water to a boil on the stove on high heat, then carefully add the corn and cook it for 3 minutes. If the corn kernels still look shiny and firm, cook the corn for another minute.

5

Use tongs to remove the corn from the hot water and place it on the plate. Allow the corn to cool for 1 minute. Touch it carefully to make sure it is not too hot.

6

Spread butter or margarine on the corn if you like. Nibble the corn straight off the cob!

21

Pancakes

Many cultures have their own kind of pancake. Early British settlers brought to the U.S. the tradition of "Pancake Tuesday," when fatty and rich ingredients were used up the day before Lent (the period before Easter). During Lent, **Christians** avoided eating rich ingredients. Today, thick and fluffy American pancakes, also called griddle cakes or flapjacks, are traditional breakfast favorites.

MAKES: 3 pancakes

PREPARATION TIME: 10 minutes

COOKING TIME: 10 minutes

FOOD VALUES: About 222 calories, 9 g of fat, 6 g of protein, and 29 g of carbohydrates per pancake.

SPECIAL DIETS: Suitable for vegetarian, nut-free, kosher, and halal diets. For vegan diets, use ¾ cup of mashed banana instead of eggs and soy milk instead of dairy milk; and for gluten-free diets, use gluten-free flour.

Equipment

- Mixing bowl
- Fork
- Wooden spoon
- Measuring cup
- Frying pan
- Spatula
- Serving plate

Ingredients

- 3 eggs
- 1 cup of milk
- 1 cup of self-rising flour (or 1 cup of plain flour mixed with 1 heaped teaspoon of baking powder)
- 1 teaspoon of cooking oil per pancake
- Maple syrup or honey to taste

What to Do

1. Crack the eggs into the mixing bowl and **beat** them with the fork until the egg whites and yolks are completely mixed.

2. Add the milk and mix with the wooden spoon.

3. Gradually add the flour a little at a time while continuing to mix, until you have a thick, smooth batter.

Mix the eggs very quickly with the fork until they are completely combined.

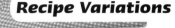

Recipe Variations

Sprinkle a few berries or a chopped banana onto the surface of the pancakes before cooking them.

Ask an adult for help with cooking and turning the pancakes.

4

Heat the frying pan on medium heat. Drizzle a teaspoon of oil into the pan. Pour half a cup of batter into the pan and cook until bubbles form on the surface and the pancake starts to look firm.

5

Loosen the pancake with the spatula and turn it over. Cook it for 1 minute more. Remove the pancake from the pan and set it on the plate. Repeat the process with the remaining batter, cooking one pancake at a time.

6

Serve the pancakes topped with maple syrup or honey.

Homemade Lemonade

Lemonade first appeared in an Arab recipe from the 1200s. It grew popular throughout Europe and arrived in the U.S. by the 1700s. Lemonade became a favorite alternative to alcohol when alcohol was banned in the early 1900s. Since then, its popularity has grown even more. During the summer, many American children make and sell lemonade for pocket money.

MAKES: 4 glasses of lemonade

PREPARATION TIME: 15 minutes

FOOD VALUES: About 80 calories and 21 g of carbohydrates per glass. No fat or protein.

SPECIAL DIETS: Suitable for vegan, vegetarian, nut-free, gluten-free, kosher, and halal diets.

Recipe Variations

Add a sprig of a fresh herb, such as mint, for a different flavor.

Make pink lemonade by adding a little red fruit juice, such as grape, raspberry, or cranberry, and a few fresh grapes or berries.

Equipment

- Cutting board
- Sharp knife
- Citrus juicer
- Bowl
- Pitcher
- Measuring cup
- Wooden spoon
- 4 glasses

Ingredients

- 6 lemons
- 3½ cups of water
- ½ cup of sugar
- 1 cup of crushed ice or ice cubes (optional)

What to Do

1 Roll each lemon on the cutting board with the palm of your hand, pressing down hard to free the juice inside.

2 Cut each lemon in half across its width. You might like to cut half of an extra lemon into thin slices to use later as a **garnish**.

3 Using the citrus juicer, squeeze the juice from the lemons into the bowl. Throw away the seeds and add the pulp to the juice.

4

Pour the water into the pitcher. Add the sugar and stir until it has completely dissolved. With an adult's help, you might like to try heating the sugar and 1 cup of water in a microwave for a minute to speed up the process.

5

Add the lemon juice to the pitcher of water. Stir thoroughly. Taste the mixture and add more water if it tastes too strong. Add more sugar if it tastes too sour.

6

Place the pitcher of lemonade in the refrigerator to chill. Before serving, add some crushed ice or ice cubes if you'd like, and garnish the pitcher or glasses with slices of lemon.

Let's Cook!

MAKES: 6–8 slices

PREPARATION TIME: 30 minutes

COOKING TIME: 45–50 minutes

FOOD VALUES: About 300 calories, 18 g of fat, 4 g of protein, and 28 g of carbohydrates per slice.

SPECIAL DIETS: Suitable for: vegetarian, nut-free, kosher, and halal diets. For gluten-free diets, use gluten-free pastry; and for vegan diets, use butter-free and egg-free filo pastry, and avoid the ice cream.

Apple Pie

The traditional American apple pie stems from the British apple pie of the 1500s, which was brought to the U.S. by the early British settlers. Unlike Dutch, French, and Swedish cooks, American cooks put spiced apples inside a closed pastry shell. They often follow family recipes, too.

Equipment

- Baking pan
- Aluminum foil
- Peeler
- Small, sharp knife
- Cutting board
- Bowl
- Wooden spoon
- Pie pan
- Oven mitts

Ingredients

- 6 firm apples
- 1 tablespoon of lemon juice
- ¾ cup of sugar (any kind)
- 2 tablespoons of plain flour
- ¾ teaspoon of ground cinnamon
- ⅛ teaspoon of ground nutmeg
- 2 sheets of ready-made pie crusts
- Ice cream

What to Do

1 Preheat the oven to 350°F. Next, line the baking pan with aluminum foil. Set aside a strip of foil that is about 0.8 inches wide for use later.

2 Peel the apples. Cut them into quarters, remove their cores, and cut each quarter farther into 3–4 thin slices about the same thickness.

3 Place the apple slices in the bowl and drizzle lemon juice over them. Add the sugar, flour, cinnamon, and nutmeg to the bowl and gently mix.

Make a peach pie instead by using peaches instead of apples.

Turn your apple pie into an apple crumble! Just scatter a crumbly topping made from ½ cup of oatmeal, ½ cup of flour, ½ cup of brown sugar, and 4 tablespoons of butter over the apple mixture instead of using the pastry sheets, then bake.

Ask an adult for help with using the knife and oven.

4

Place one sheet of pie crust over the pie pan and press it gently into place from the center out.

5

Fill the pie crust with the apple mixture, then top the apple mixture with the second pie crust. Roll the edges of the pie crusts together using your fingers. Pinch them into a pattern if you'd like. Cut slits into the top of the pie crust to let steam escape while baking.

6

Cover the edge of the pie with foil to prevent it from burning. Next, place the pie pan on the baking pan and bake for 30 minutes.

7

After 30 minutes, take the pie out of the oven, using oven mitts. Take the foil off the edge of the pie and return the pie to the oven. Take it out again when the pie crust is golden (about 15–20 minutes). Let the pie cool, then cut it into slices and serve with ice cream.

An American Food Celebration: Thanksgiving

Thanksgiving is a harvest festival celebrated by Americans all over the world. It is a time when families and friends gather and eat a special feast of traditional American foods.

What Is Thanksgiving?

Thanksgiving is an American holiday that falls on the fourth Thursday in November. It is held in memory of a fall harvest feast shared by the first British settlers, known as the Pilgrims, and their Native American neighbors in 1621, one year after the Pilgrims had landed in Plymouth, Massachusetts.

How Is Thanksgiving Celebrated?

Many American families travel long distances to meet for a special Thanksgiving dinner. They may watch football games together. American cities may also hold parades or public processions, such as the Macy's Thanksgiving Day Parade, which is televised nationally. It features marching bands, huge floats, and enormous balloons, often of cartoon characters. The parade traditionally ends with a Santa Claus float, marking the start of the Christmas season.

The most well-known parade is the Macy's Thanksgiving Day Parade, held in New York City.

Food

The highlight of the Thanksgiving dinner is a stuffed, roast turkey, usually served with cranberry sauce, mashed potatoes and gravy, sweet potatoes, corn, and other fall vegetables. The meal usually ends with pumpkin or pecan pie. These foods are native to the U.S. and were introduced to the early settlers by the Native Americans. Migrant groups often add their own specialties to the feast. Italian Americans may include lasagne and Chinese Americans may **marinate** the turkey in soy sauce and ginger.

The National Thanksgiving Turkey Presentation

Every Thanksgiving, the National Turkey Federation presents a live turkey to the American president. The president then "pardons" this turkey so that it can live out its natural life.

A Thanksgiving feast includes traditional American foods, such as pie and roast turkey.

Try This!

Cooking is a creative skill you can enjoy every day. Try these activities and learn more about cooking American food.

- Carve a pumpkin into a jack-o'-lantern for Halloween. Toast and salt the pumpkin seeds, and eat them as a snack.

- Start your own American garden by growing chilies, miniature tomatoes, pumpkins, and sweet corn. Take photos of the vegetables as they grow. Find recipes that use them.

- Search for interesting American recipes on the Internet, such as snickerdoodles and s'mores. Make them for a treat.

- If you enjoy hot and spicy food, ask your parents to buy a jar of American chili sauce as a treat. Be warned, it's hot!

- Find an American recipe that uses a vegetable or fruit that is new to you. Cook it!

- The states of Hawaii and Alaska have some exciting regional specialties. Explore one of these and find your favorite. Can you make it?

- Celebrate an American holiday by decorating a cake with an American flag made with blueberries and strawberries on cream. You could also create a red, white, and blue fruit salad with strawberries, blueberries, and chunks of apple sprinkled with lemon juice.

- Collect your favourite American recipes from the Internet or local library and create your own cookbook.

Glossary

allergic
having an allergy, or a bad reaction to certain foods

calories
units measuring the amount of energy food provides

carbohydrates
substances that provide the body with energy

Christians
people who follow the teachings of Jesus Christ

climate
the general weather conditions of an area

continent
one of seven large landmasses on Earth, usually containing many countries and surrounded by water

culture
the ways of living that a group of people has developed over time

diets
foods and drinks normally consumed by different people or groups of people

economy
the system of trade by which a country makes and uses its wealth

fertile
capable of producing good crops

garnish
a small amount of a certain food used to add flavor or color to a dish

gluten
a protein found in wheat and some other grains that makes dough springy

Jews
people who follow the religion of Judaism

Latin Americans
people from South or Central America

marinate
soak in a mixture of herbs, oils, and spices to add flavor to food

migration
the movement of people to a new place to live

Muslims
people who follow the religion of Islam

native
living or growing naturally in a place

Native American
relating to the indigenous peoples of North, South, or Central America, but especially of the North

nutritious
providing nutrients, or nourishment

protein
a nutrient that helps bodies grow and heal

slaves
people who are owned by other people and are forced to work for them

staple food
a food that is eaten regularly and is one of the main parts of a diet

swamps
areas of wet, soft land

traditions
patterns of behavior handed down through generations

Index